MW01171372

MOMMY WHO IS GOD?

by

Paula Arceneaux-Ware

ISBN: 9781693428173

Dedication

This book is a special edition (2nd) to the original book MOMMY WHO IS GOD? dedicated to my dear husband and sweet daughter. It is based on a real-life experience when our daughter was 4 years old. She approached me with this question, which is the title of the book. I was so stunned and shocked that I was speechless. This question changed our lives!

Throughout this short story, I had to think and act quickly so that I did not lose our daughter's interest and attention. I shared the basics with her to show her just how amazing God really is and how loving He is to all of His children. His love includes everything He made, which is EVERYTHING!

I thank God for bringing me back to Him through our sweet daughter! I pray everyone enjoys the story, the prayers and the activity book.

Thank you for supporting what God has given me as an author.

God bless you!

Editor: Mrs. Judith Young, CEO of College Excellence
[www.collegeexcellence.com]

4

One Sunday morning, Zoe skipped toward her mother with a question.

She said, "Mommy, who is God?" Her mother was shock<u>ed</u> and gasp<u>ed</u> for air! She was speech<u>less</u>. She couldn't close her mouth.

---

shocked - a sudden or violent disturbance of the mind, emotions, or sensibilities
gasped - to catch one's breath
speechless - absence or loss of speech

Zoe was confus<u>ed</u> because her mother's eyes were filled with tear drops as she kneel<u>ed</u> on the floor.

"Mommy?", Zoie whispered. Her mother whimper<u>ed</u> as she said, "Yes, Baby Girl?"

Zoe could tell something was wrong. "Mommy, are you alright?"

---

confused - difficult to understand
kneeled - to go down on one or both knees
whimpered - to cry with low sounds

Her mother wiped her tears away. They hugged each other tightly and sat on the floor. "I'm sorry, Zoe. Mommy was just surprised by your question. I didn't realize you didn't know about God."

Her mother spoke with joy! "God created us! He created the earth! He created animals! He created EVERYTHING!"

---

tightly - firmly held in place
surprised - a sudden feeling of wonder
created - to make or construct something

They stood up and twirled around the living room. Zoe's mother started chanting, "God is good! Thank you Father! God is good! Thank you Father!"

Then they skipped into Zoe's bedroom. Her mother began explaining that God is our Father and He loves us. "He created us and everything in your room. He even created Fluffy!"

---

twirled - to spin or rotate rapidly
chanting - to sing
explaining - to make clear

Her mother was so excited she started to dance! She said, "God made the flowers, trees, grass, sun, and the wind!"

Zoe smiled with glee and said, "He sounds amazing! When can I meet Him?"

Zoe's mother said, "Let's go inside to find Mommy's Bible. We can learn all about Him...together."

---

started - to begin motion
glee - expressing joy
bible - sacred writings by Christians

The scriptures that follow should be prayed with the children we love and serve.

Please take time to explain the meaning of the scriptures and the value they have in our lives.

It is our responsibility to teach our children who God is and how much He loves us. From my experience, the earlier we share the word of God with our children, the sooner they embrace Him.

Thank you for taking time to support the spiritual growth of our future leaders!

Peace and Love in Jesus' Name

I AM WITH YOU
ALWAYS

James 1:17

The Lord's Prayer

Matthew 6:9-13

9 This, then, is how you should pray:
"Our Father in heaven,
hallowed be your name,
10 your kingdom come, your will be done,
on earth as it is in heaven.
11 Give us today our daily bread.
12 And forgive us our debts, as we also
have forgiven our debtors.
13 And lead us not into temptation, but
deliver us from the evil one."

Date learned by heart:

_____

Prayer for Strength

Phillipians 4:13

I can do all things through Him who
strengthens me.

Date learned by heart:

_____

Prayer for Courage

Joshua 1:9

Have I not commanded you?
Be strong and courageous.
Do not be frightened,
and do not be dismayed,
for the Lord your God is with you
wherever you go.

Date learned by heart:

_____

Prayer for Peace

Phillipians 4:6

Do not be anxious about anything, but in everything by prayer and supplication with thanksgiving let your requests be made known to God.

Date learned by heart:

_____

Prayer for Provision

Phillipians 4:19

And my God will supply every need of yours
according to His riches in
glory in Christ Jesus.

Date learned by heart:

_____

Prayer for Direction

Proverbs 3:5-6

5 Trust in the Lord with all your heart, and do not lean on your own understanding;
6 in all your ways acknowledge Him, and He will make straight your paths.

Date learned by heart:

_____

Prayer for Protection

Psalm 91:1-2

1 He who dwells in the shelter of the Most
High will abide in the
shadow of the Almighty.
2 I will say to the Lord, "My refuge
and my fortress,
my God in whom I trust."

Date learned by heart:

_____

Prayer for Joy

Psalm 16:11

You make known to me the path of life,
in your presence there is fullness of joy;
at your right hand are pleasures
forevermore.

Date learned by heart:

_____

Prayer for Compassion

Ephesians 4:32

Be kind to one another, tenderhearted,
forgiving one another,
as God in Christ forgave you.

Date learned by heart:

_____

Prayer for Justice

Isaiah 1:17

Learn to do good; seek justice,
correct oppression,
bring justice to the fatherless,
plead the widow's cause.

Date learned by heart:

_____

Prayer for Wisdom

James 1:5

If any of you lacks wisdom,
let him ask God,
who gives generously to all
without reproach,
and it will be given.

Date learned by heart:

_____

Prayer for Hope

Romans 15:13

May the God of hope fill you with all joy and
peace in believing,
so that by the power of the Holy Spirit
you may abound in hope.

Date learned by heart:

_____

Prayer for Love

2 Corinthians 13

Love is patient and kind,
love does not envy or boast,
it is not arrogant or rude,
it does not insist on its own way,
it is not irritable or resentful;
it does not rejoice at wrongdoing, but
rejoices with the truth.
Love bears all things, believes all things,
hopes all things, endures all things.
Love never ends.

Date learned by heart:

_____

I KNEW YOU BEFORE I formed YOU IN YOUR MOTHER'S WOMB. BEFORE YOU WERE BORN I SET YOU apart.

JEREMIAH 1:5

Wonderfully Made!

Psalm 127:3 Behold, children are a
heritage from the Lord, the fruit of the
womb a reward.

If you enjoyed this book, please share it with your family and friends. Let's connect with other brothers and sisters to spread God's love.

For more information or to book the author,

Paula Arceneaux-Ware, please visit

[www.iampware.com].

 @iampware

 @iampware

 IamPWare

Made in the USA
Columbia, SC
17 July 2022

63585163R00020